MEXICAN MARVELS

Up to Date Travel Guide to
Exploring the Wonders of Mexico

Hugo Denise

CONTENTS

INTRODUCTION

About Mexico

Mexico, a land of contrasts and cultural treasures, invites you on an enthralling journey that defies time and tradition. Mexico, located in southern North America, effortlessly blends its ancient roots with the vibrant energy of the present.

Historical Riches

Mexico's heart is a tapestry woven with the threads of ancient civilizations. From the ruins of the Aztec capital, Tenochtitlan, to the enigmatic Teotihuacan pyramids, history reverberates through every stone and monument. Explore the Mayan wonders of Chichen Itza and Palenque, where majestic pyramids rise, whispering tales of a bygone era.

Diverse Cultures

The cultural landscape of Mexico is a celebration of diversity. Indigenous traditions, deeply rooted in ancient practices, coexist with Spanish colonization. From the vibrant markets of Oaxaca to the colonial charm of Guanajuato, each region has its own distinct identity. Dive into the kaleidoscope of languages, music, dance, and art that define Mexico's cultural mosaic.

Natural Splendors

Mexico's natural beauty captivates visitors in addition to its cultural riches. Every landscape, from the golden beaches of Cancun to the dense jungles of Chiapas, exemplifies the country's geographical diversity. Discover Baja California's arid deserts, the Yucatán Peninsula's biodiversity, and the snow-capped peaks of the Sierra Madre.

Culinary Delights

Mexican cuisine, recognized by UNESCO as an Intangible Cultural Heritage, is a sensory journey. Enjoy the spicy delights of street tacos, the rich flavors of Puebla's mole, and the freshness of ceviche along the coastal stretches. Every dish tells a story, a tale of indigenous ingredients mingled with European influences.

Warm Hospitality

But, more than the landscapes and flavors, the warmth of the Mexican people leaves an indelible impression. Mexicans are known for their hospitality and genuine friendliness, and they welcome visitors with open arms, inviting them to join in the joyous fiestas, lively celebrations, and simple pleasures of everyday life.

When to Visit

Mexico is a year-round travel destination because of its varied landscapes, lively culture, and extensive history. Explore historic sites, unwind on immaculate beaches, or take part in regional celebrations—every season has something special to offer.

1. Peak Season (December to April)

Why Visit: Take advantage of the best weather during Mexico's high season, which is typically dry and pleasant. Beach lovers will love coastal areas like Cancún and Puerto Vallarta. The pleasant weather in Mexico City and the surrounding areas makes it the perfect place to explore the local cultures.

2. Spring (March-May)

Why Visit: Springtime brings pleasant weather and verdant surroundings. It's a great time of year to explore archaeological sites and engage in outdoor activities without the crowds. Events like Holy Week's Semana Santa allow one to immerse oneself in another culture.

3. Summer (June to August)

Why Visit: Bask in the colorful energy of Mexico's summertime. For beach lovers, coastal areas are ideal, and mountainous areas provide relief from the heat. But be ready for the odd downpour of rain, especially in the afternoons.

4. Rainy Season (June to October) R

Why Visit: The rainy season offers benefits even in spite of sporadic downpours. The scenery becomes verdant and lush, and with fewer visitors come more private experiences. This is a potentially rewarding season if you appreciate the vibrancy of nature and are adaptable to your outdoor plans.

5. Fall (September to November)

Why Visit: With its combination of lush landscapes and the end of the rainy season, fall is a great time to go for nature lovers. Additionally, there are fewer tourists during this time, making for more private encounters. The cultural significance lies in the celebration of the Day of the Dead in late October/early November.

6. Low Season: (September to mid-December)

Why Visit: Enjoy the off-season when there are fewer crowds and cheaper prices. For low cost travelers who wish to visit Mexico without having to pay peak-season prices, now is a great time. There may be sporadic rainfall in some areas.

7. Cultural Festivals (Throughout the Year)

Why Visit: Mexico holds a lot of cultural festivals all year long. You can organize your trip around these colorful events for a fully immersive experience, whether it's the Day of the Dead celebrations in November, the Guelaguetza in Oaxaca, or regional fiestas.

8. Winter (December to February)

Why Visit: There's a good reason why winter is the busiest time of year. Take pleasure in the festive atmosphere, pleasant temperatures, and clear skies. Winter offers a fantastic backdrop for exploring historic sites, enjoying beach resorts, and indulging in culinary delights.

9. Whale Watching (December to April)

Why Go: If you want to go whale watching, schedule your trip for between December and April. During these months, Baja California is renowned for its breathtaking whale migrations, which provide a singular wildlife experience.

10. Adventure Activities (Year-Round)

Why Visit: Because of its varied terrain, Mexico offers adventure activities all year round. Regardless of the season, there are exciting things to do, like hiking in the Copper Canyon or discovering cenotes in the Yucatán.

Essential Travel Tips

In order to ensure a smooth and enriching experience during your exploration of Mexican Marvels, keep in mind these essential travel tips.

1. Weather Awareness

Mexico experiences a variety of climates. Consider the season and region you'll be exploring when packing. Lightweight clothing, sunscreen, and a hat are essential, especially in coastal areas.

2. Currency and Payment

The official currency of Mexico is the Mexican Peso (MXN). Be sure to check the current exchange rates and carry some local currency for small purchases. While credit cards are widely accepted in urban areas, cash is essential in more remote areas.

3. Language Basics

Even though many Mexicans in tourist locations speak English, it's still beneficial to learn a few simple Spanish words. The effort is appreciated by the locals, and in less visited areas, it can be very beneficial.

4. Safety Precautions

Put your safety first by keeping up with the most recent travel advisories for particular areas. Make sure you use reliable transportation, keep an eye on your possessions, and stay away from remote areas at night.

5. Health Considerations

Before visiting Mexico, find out if there are any vaccinations you need to get. Keep yourself hydrated and carry a basic first aid kit, especially in warmer climates. Before your trip, speak with your healthcare provider if you have any specific health concerns.

6. Local Etiquette and Customs

Honor regional traditions and customs. Remember to be courteous in return, as Mexicans are renowned for their warmth and hospitality. Acquire knowledge of cultural customs, like salutations and table manners, to effortlessly maneuver through social gatherings.

7. Transportation Tips

Look into Mexican transportation options. Buses are affordable and scenic for shorter trips, domestic flights are effective for covering large distances, and rental cars offer flexibility for seeing off-the-beaten-path locations.

8. Street Food Caution

Accept Mexico's diverse food culture, but use caution when consuming street food. Choosing suppliers with a high customer turnover rate indicates that their products are safe and up to date. Consume purified or bottled water to prevent health problems.

9. Electricity and Adapters

Mexico uses 120V, 60Hz standard North American power outlets. Remember to pack the chargers and adapters you'll need for your electronics.

10. Cultural Sensitivity

Pay attention to regional traditions, particularly those practiced by indigenous people. Request permission before taking pictures, show reverence for holy places, and engage in cultural events humbly.

11. Travel Insurance

Invest in comprehensive travel insurance that includes coverage for lost luggage, medical emergencies, and trip cancellations. Make sure you have access to nearby medical facilities and emergency contact information.

12. Connect with Locals

Talk to people in the area to improve your experience. Take part in market visits, festivals, and local events. Developing relationships with the residents frequently results in unique and genuine experiences.

How to Get There

By Air

Flying is the most popular and practical way to travel to Mexico. Mexico has excellent international connections thanks to its large airports, which are located in cities like Guadalajara, Cancún, and Mexico City. There are many airlines that offer flights to and from Mexico, with a variety of options to fit your needs and price range. To ensure the best prices and convenient schedules, make sure to book your flights well in advance.

International Airports

Serving the nation's capital, Mexico City International Airport (MEX) is a significant hub for international travel.

The gateway to the Riviera Maya and the Yucatán Peninsula is Cancún International Airport (CUN).

Guadalajara Miguel Hidalgo y Costilla International Airport (GDL) connects Guanajuato and beyond's cultural treasures.

By Land

Consider going to Mexico by land if you're already in a neighboring country or if you just want a beautiful trip. The nation has wide borders with Belize and Guatemala to the south, and the United States to the north. Overland travel options are provided by bus services, private vehicles, and organized tours.

By Sea

Travelers who enjoy taking cruises may also decide to reach Mexico by sea. Cruise ships from all over the world call at major ports like Cozumel, Puerto Vallarta, and Cabo San Lucas. Cruises give you a different viewpoint and let you discover hidden coastal treasures and popular tourist destinations.

Local Transportation

When you get to Mexico, you'll discover that the nation has an efficient transportation system. There are plenty of domestic flights, buses, and rental cars available.

Domestic flights are the most efficient way to travel large distances, but buses are a more affordable and visually appealing choice for shorter trips. You can travel at your own speed and discover off-the-beaten-path locations thanks to the flexibility of rental cars.

Travel Tips

Make sure your passport is up to date, and find out what kind of visa you need according to your country.

It can save you time and money to book flights and other travel-related services in advance, especially during the busiest travel seasons.

To prevent any issues upon arrival, familiarize yourself with customs regulations.

It is easy to visit particular regions thanks to Mexico's vast network of regional buses and airplanes.

PLANNING YOUR TRIP

Recommended Itineraries

1. Historical Magnificence (10 Days)

Day 1–3: Mexico City

Admire the ancient Teotihuacan ruins, stroll through the historic center, and go to the National Museum of Anthropology.

Day 4- 6: Oaxaca

Savor the regional cuisine, explore the Monte Albán archaeological site, and become fully immersed in Oaxaca's rich indigenous culture.

Day 7–10: Chichen Itza and Merida

Explore the famous Chichen Itza Mayan ruins and take in Merida's colonial charm.

2. Coastal Paradise (7 Days)

Day 1- 3 Cancún and Playa del Carmen

Unwind on the immaculate beaches, go snorkeling in the glistening waters, and take in the exciting nightlife.

Day 4-5: Tulum

Unwind on Tulum's bohemian beaches and explore the historic ruins perched on the cliff.

Day 6–7: Cozumel

On the island of Cozumel, take snorkeling and diving excursions to explore the colorful underwater world.

3. Culinary Adventure (14 Days)

Day 1–4: Mexico City

Take advantage of market visits, street food tours, and dining at well-known restaurants to fully experience the varied culinary scene.

Days 5-7: Puebla

Discover the gastronomic legacy of Puebla, which is renowned for its mole poblano and authentic Mexican pastries.

Days 8–10: Oaxaca

Explore the flavors of Oaxaca, known for its mezcal and intricate moles.

Day 11–14: Guadalajara and Tequila

Savor the cuisine of Guadalajara and take a Tequila tasting excursion among the agave fields nearby.

4. Nature and Adventure (12 Days)

Day 1–3: Puerto Vallarta

In Puerto Vallarta, get started with aquatic activities and jungle exploration.

Day 4- 6: Guanajuato

Explore Guanajuato's underground streets and head out onto the nearby hiking trails.

Day 7-9: Chiapas

Discover the area's natural treasures, such as the Agua Azul waterfalls and Sumidero Canyon.

Day 10–12: Cabo San Lucas

Enjoy aquatic activities and marine excursions in the picturesque surroundings of Cabo San Lucas to cap off your adventure.

Budgeting and Costs

1. Accommodation

There are a variety of lodging options available in Mexico, ranging from opulent resorts to affordable hostels. While mid-range hotels may cost between $80-$150 per night, budget travelers can typically find cozy options for $30–$60. Expensive resorts charge more than $200 per night.

2. Transportation

The cost of transportation varies depending on the route you select. Depending on the distance, domestic flights between major cities normally cost between $50 and $200. Buses that travel longer distances are less expensive; their fares range from $10 to $50. Without fuel, a car rental can run you $30 to $50 per day.

3. Food and Dining

The varied and reasonably priced cuisine of Mexico is one of its delights. Meals at local restaurants and street food vendors are reasonably priced, ranging from $5 to $10. While upscale dining establishments can cost more than

$50 per person, mid-range restaurants may only charge $15 to $30 per person.

4. Activities and Excursions

Different attractions and activities have different admission costs. Aim to spend between $10 and $30 on museum admission, $20 to $40 on guided tours, and extra for adventure activities like hiking, diving, or snorkeling.

5. Local Transportation

With fares ranging from $0.50 to $2 per ride, public transportation—such as buses and metro systems—is reasonably priced. There are taxis available; the cost varies depending on the location and distance. Ride-sharing services present cost-effective and practical choices.

6. Miscellaneous Expenses: Include miscellaneous expenses like 10%–15% gratuities for service providers, SIM cards for local communication (roughly $10–$20), and any unforeseen expenses. Maintaining a small emergency fund for unanticipated events is advised.

7. Currency Exchange

The Mexican Peso (MXN) is the accepted form of payment. Keep an eye on exchange rates prior to your trip as they may change. Banks, currency exchange offices, and airports all offer currency exchange services. In cities, credit cards are commonly accepted.

Tips for Budget Travel

For genuine and reasonably priced meals, check out the street food markets and neighborhood restaurants.

If you travel during shoulder seasons, you can save money on lodging and activities.

To reduce your travel costs, choose shared rides, buses, and metro systems.

Entry Requirements

1. Passport

Every visitor to Mexico needs to have a current passport. Make sure your passport is valid for at least six months after the date you plan to travel.

2. Visa Requirements

For stays of up to 180 days for tourism and business, citizens of many nations—including the US, Canada, the EU, and many Latin American nations—do not need a visa. Verify the necessary visa for your country of residence and the intended purpose of your trip.

3. Tourist Card (FMM)

Most visitors must obtain a Tourist Card, also called an FMM (Forma Migratoria Múltiple), even if they do not require a visa. You can spend up to 180 days in Mexico with this card. The FMM is available online, at the port of entry, and through Mexican consulates overseas.

4. Border Zone Exception

Visitors who spend less than 72 hours in border zones, such as Tijuana and Ciudad Juarez, may not need to obtain an FMM. For confirmation of your eligibility for the border zone exception, check with the Mexican immigration authorities.

5. Departure Tax

As of my most recent update in 2023, passengers departing Mexico via air are not subject to a departure tax. The price of your airline ticket usually includes this fee.

Tips

A copy of your passport, FMM, and any other pertinent travel documents should be kept in a safe place.

Make sure you correctly complete the FMM and save the bottom half of the document; you will need it when you leave Mexico.

Health and Safety Guidelines

1. Travel Insurance

Purchase comprehensive travel insurance that includes coverage for lost luggage, medical emergencies, and trip cancellations.

2. Health Precautions

Before traveling to Mexico, inquire with your healthcare provider about any recommended vaccinations. Make sure your coverage lasts the whole time you are in the country. Bring along basic first aid supplies, necessary prescription drugs, and essential medications.

3. Food and Water Safety

To prevent foodborne illnesses, only drink bottled or purified water. When choosing a street food vendor, exercise caution and choose those who maintain proper hygiene. Peel fruits when possible, or go with cooked foods.

4. Personal Safety

Watch out for your possessions, particularly in busy places and popular tourist destinations. Keep valuables in hotel safes and keep pricey stuff out of sight.

5. Local Emergency Services

Learn the location of the closest hospitals or clinics as well as the local emergency services number, which is 911 in most of Mexico. Make a list of emergency contacts that include the embassy or consulate of your nation.

6. Altitude Considerations

Be mindful of the possibility of altitude sickness if your travels take you to high-altitude locations like Mexico City. Drink plenty of water, abstain from alcohol, and give your body time to adjust.

7. Sun Protection

The sun in Mexico can be very strong, particularly near the coast. To prevent sunburn and dehydration, apply sunscreen, wear protective clothes, and maintain hydration.

8. Transportation Safety

Select reliable modes of transportation. Check the safety requirements for ridesharing, taxis, and buses.

9. Local Customs and Laws

Become familiar with local customs and laws to ensure polite and legal behavior. Respect any special rules that may apply, particularly in places of worship or cultural significance.

10. Emergency Preparedness

Make a plan for potential emergencies, which should include a communication plan with fellow travelers. Give someone you trust a copy of your itinerary and make sure they are aware of your whereabouts.

11. Weather Preparation

Learn about the local weather in the areas you'll be visiting. Be prepared for varying weather conditions by packing appropriately and keeping up with any impending natural disasters, like hurricanes or tropical storms.

Top Historical Landmarks

1. Teotihuacan

Admire Teotihuacan, an ancient city that once housed the famous Pyramids of the Sun and Moon. The sophisticated urban design and architecture of pre-Columbian civilizations are on display in this archaeological marvel.

2. Chichen Itza

Discover Chichen Itza, a UNESCO World Heritage Site and one of the New Seven Wonders of the World, by traveling to the center of the Yucatan Peninsula. Admire the old ball court and the Kukulkan Pyramid's accuracy.

3. Palenque

Discover the enigmas of Palenque by submerging yourself in the verdant jungles of Chiapas. The elaborate architecture of this Mayan city is on display in the Temple of Inscriptions, which is home to the tomb of the illustrious Pakal the Great.

4. Templo Mayor

Discover Templo Mayor, the principal temple of Aztecs, by taking a stroll through the center of Mexico City. Discover more about Aztec daily life and religious customs by touring the nearby museum and archaeological sites.

5. Monte Albán

Visit the mountain ridge-perched archaeological site of Monte Albán in Oaxaca. This historic Zapotec city has striking buildings like the Great Plaza and the Observatory, as well as expansive views.

6. Palacio Nacional

Take a tour of the Palacio Nacional while you're standing in Mexico City's famed Zócalo. Discover the intricate history of Mexico through Diego Rivera's murals, which span from the Aztecs to the Mexican Revolution.

7. Guanajuato

Wander through the quaint streets of Guanajuato, a colonial city that was vital to Mexico's struggle for independence. See Diego Rivera's birthplace and the Alhóndiga de Granaditas.

8. Castillo de Chapultepec

To get to the castle with a fascinating history, climb Chapultepec Hill. Take a tour of its halls, which have housed the president, the military academy, and the imperial residence.

9. Templo de Santo Domingo (Oaxaca)

Take in the opulence of this baroque structure in Oaxaca. Admire the church's and the Santo Domingo Cultural Center's elaborate details.

10. Uxmal

Uncover the wonder of Uxmal, located on the Yucatan Peninsula. Admire the Puuc-style architecture of the Governor's Palace and the Pyramid of the Magician.

Must-Try Cuisines

1. Tacos

Savor tacos, which are the ultimate street food. These folded delights are a true taste of Mexican street culture, whether they are filled with tender carne asada, al pastor, carnitas, or grilled vegetables.

2. Guacamole

Slurp up some freshly made guacamole, which is a delicious concoction of ripe avocados, lime juice, tomatoes, onions, cilantro, and salt. Combine it with crunchy tortilla chips to create the ideal starter.

3. Mole Poblano

Soak up the nuanced tastes of this rich, velvety sauce, which is made with chocolate, chili peppers, spices, and other ingredients. Savor it with turkey or chicken for a classic Mexican meal.

4. Chiles en Nogada

Savor the national dish chiles en nogada, which consists of stuffed poblano peppers with a blend of fruits and meats, covered in a walnut cream sauce, and crowned with pomegranate seeds.

5. Tamales

Savor the deliciousness of tamales, which are masa parcels that are steamed and filled with a variety of savory or sweet fillings. Every taste is a flavor explosion, whether it's pineapple and cinnamon or chicken and mole.

6. Ceviche

This dish of marinated raw fish or shellfish, usually cured in lime or lemon juice and combined with tomatoes, onions, cilantro, and chili peppers, will revive your palate.

7. Pozole

A bowl of this robust soup, which is made with hominy, meat (typically chicken or pork), and a variety of spices, will warm your soul. Add oregano, lettuce, lime, and radishes on top.

8. Street Corn (Elote)

Give in to the mouthwatering taste of grilled corn on the cob drenched in mayonnaise, cotija cheese, chili powder, and lime juice. Every bite is a symphony of flavors.

9. Enchiladas

Savor the comforting taste of enchiladas, which are rolled tortillas stuffed with cheese, meat, or beans and covered in a delicious chili sauce. Add some shredded lettuce, queso fresco, and sour cream as garnish.

10. Sopes

Enjoy the robust sopes, which are thick cornmeal patties topped with meat, lettuce, salsa, crumbled cheese, and refried beans. There's a delightful mix of textures in every bite.

Art and Culture

Lose yourself in the colorful tapestry of Mexican art and culture. Examine the creative manifestations and traditional practices that characterize this fascinating country.

1. Muralism

Explore the world of Mexican muralism, a movement spearheaded by well-known artists like Jose Clemente Orozco, Diego Rivera, and David Alfaro Siqueiros. Admire the enormous murals that paint Mexico's history, hardships, and victories in public areas.

2. Frida Kahlo

Explore the mysterious realm of one of Mexico's most renowned artists, Frida Kahlo. Visit the Frida Kahlo Museum (Casa Azul) in Mexico City to learn about her life and work. Her colorful self-portraits and personal items tell a story of tenacity and inventiveness.

3. Alebrijes

Discover the colorful, folk art sculptures known as alebrijes, which transport you to a whimsical world. Mexican artisans showcase their creativity and imagination through these fantastic creatures, which are often crafted from carved wood and painted with intricate designs.

4. Day of the Dead (Día de los Muertos)

The Day of the Dead, also known as Día de los Muertos, is a deeply cultural celebration where families honor and remember their departed loved ones. Take in intricate altars, colorful sugar skulls, and processions that perfectly represent life and death.

5. Traditional Music and Dance

Allow the beats of Mexican traditional music and dance to take you to various parts of the nation. Every performance showcases the diversity of Mexican culture, from the complex footwork of folkloric dances to the upbeat beats of mariachi in Jalisco.

6. Contemporary Art Scene

Explore Mexico's contemporary art scene, which features galleries and shows that feature the creations of contemporary Mexican artists. The current state-of-the-art world is full of interesting sculptures and inventive installations.

CANCÚN AND THE YUCATÁN
PENINSULA

Mayan Ruins

Explore the historic wonders of Mayan civilization as you go on an enthralling voyage through time. Explore the majesty and enigma of the Mayan ruins strewn throughout the Yucatán Peninsula.

1. Chichen Itza

See the famous Pyramid of Kukulkan at Chichen Itza, one of the New Seven Wonders of the World and a UNESCO World Heritage Site. Discover this masterpiece of archaeology, which includes the Great Ball Court, the Temple of the Warriors, and the Sacred Cenote.

2. Tulum

Admire Tulum's breathtaking coastline, which combines the Caribbean Sea's turquoise waves with historic ruins. Discover the remarkably preserved buildings, such as El Castillo and the Temple of the Frescoes, which provide an insight into the way of life of the Maya seafarers.

3. Coba

Explore the ancient city of Coba by taking a jungle expedition. Scale the massive Nohoch Mul pyramid for sweeping views of the Yucatán, and discover the system of sacbeob, or white roads, that links Coba's various buildings.

4. Ek Balam

Discover the undiscovered jewel of Ek Balam, renowned for the imposing Acropolis and its exquisite stucco sculptures. Admire the exquisite entrance arch and the preserved hieroglyphics, which demonstrate the Mayas' mastery of art.

5. Uxmal

Enter Uxmal's Puuc-style architecture, which features elaborate geometric patterns. See the Governor's Palace, the Pyramid of the Magician, and the Nuns' Quadrangle, which showcase the Maya's artistic and astronomical prowess.

6. Calakmul

Explore the grandeur of Calakmul, one of the biggest ancient Maya cities, by delving deeply into the Calakmul Biosphere Reserve. To get amazing views of the surrounding jungle, climb the large pyramid.

Top Beaches

1. Cancún's Playa Delfines

Enjoy Playa Delfines' splendor, which is renowned for its long stretches of snow-white sand and vivid turquoise waters. Admire the soft waves and take in expansive views of the Caribbean Sea.

2. Tulum Beach

Unwind on Tulum Beach's bohemian-chic shores, where sugary sands and crystal-clear waters meet. Discover seaside cenotes and take in the views of the historic Mayan ruins.

3. Playa Norte, Isla Mujeres

Savor the peace and quiet of Isla Mujeres' Playa Norte. This beach is a relaxing haven with its serene waters and swaying palm trees. Take in the relaxed atmosphere while snorkeling in the crystal-clear waters.

4. Akumal Beach, Akumal

Discover the splendor of Akumal Beach, which is well-known for its calm marine turtles. Savor the tranquil atmosphere of this coastal treasure while snorkeling in the protected bay, which is teeming with marine life.

5. Xpu-Ha Beach, Riviera Maya

Take in the breathtaking scenery at this undiscovered haven on the Riviera Maya. Savor the powder-soft sands, crystal-clear waters, and the verdant Yucatán jungle backdrop.

6. Playacar Beach, Playa del Carmen

Stroll along Playacar Beach, which is renowned for its posh atmosphere. Savor the coastal charm, stroll around the lively Fifth Avenue nearby, and unwind beneath the palm trees' shade.

7. Xcacel Beach, Xcacel

Explore the untouched splendor of Xcacel Beach, a turtle sanctuary boasting a spotless coastline. Discover the natural beauties of this isolated sanctuary and get away from the crowds.

8. Playa Akumal, Akumal

Take in the peace and quiet of Playa Akumal, where white sands and Caribbean turquoise waters converge. Take in the tranquil atmosphere while lounging on beachside palapas and snorkeling with sea turtles.

9. Mahahual Beach, Mahahual

Discover the relaxed atmosphere of this undiscovered Costa Maya jewel, Mahahual Beach. Enjoy the seafood that is locally produced, take a stroll along the malecón, and relax in this seaside town's rustic charm.

10. Holbox Beach, Isla Holbox

Travel to Holbox Beach, a bohemian haven. For those looking for a quiet beach experience, this island getaway with its fine white sand and glistening clear waters offers a peaceful haven.

OAXACA

Explore Rich Indigenous Heritage

1. Zapotec Archaeological Sites

Visits to historic Zapotec archaeological sites like Monte Albán and Mitla are a great way to start your exploration. Admire the magnificent architecture and dexterous stone carvings that showcase the Zapotec civilization's rich past.

2. Oaxacan Textiles in Teotitlán del Valle

Get lost in Teotitlan del Valle's Oaxacan textile universe. See how elaborate rugs are woven by hand using age-old methods and natural dyes that have been passed down through the generations.

3. Guelaguetza Festiva

Arrange your trip to coincide with the Guelaguetza Festival, a colorful July celebration of Oaxacan culture. Discover the vibrant costumes, lively dances, and festive atmosphere as various indigenous communities unite to celebrate their cultural heritage.

4. Alebrijes Art in San Martín Tilcajete

Discover San Martín Tilcajete, a village famous for its fanciful, colorful wood-carved creatures known as alebrijes. Watch the talented artisans at work as they give these one-of-a-kind creations life.

5. Oaxaca City Markets:

Explore the city's thriving marketplaces, including Mercado 20 de Noviembre and Mercado Benito Juárez. Meet local vendors offering handicrafts, textiles, and regional specialties.

6. Mezcal Production in Matatlán

Learn about the age-old craft of Matatlán mezcal production. See the elaborate process of fermenting and distilling agave, which is a deeply ingrained Oaxacan indigenous tradition, by visiting nearby mezcalerías.

7. Zapotec Cuisine in Etla

Take pleasure in Etla's Zapotec cuisine. Taste traditional dishes like tlayudas, molotes, and memelas that highlight the region's culinary heritage and peruse local markets for unusual ingredients.

8. Zapotec Weaving in Santo Tomás Jalieza

Take a closer look at the Zapotec weaving culture in Santo Tomás Jalieza. Observe the production of elaborate accessories and textiles, such as colorful huipiles and finely woven belts, which demonstrate the community's commitment to maintaining its craft.

Traditional Crafts

1. Oaxacan Alebrijes

Enter the enchanted world of Oaxacan alebrijes, which are amazing wooden creatures that are hand-carved and painted in vibrant hues and intricate patterns. Discover Oaxaca's native craftspeople who bring the region's Zapotec customs to life through these wacky creations.

2. Textiles

Teotitlán del Valle is a village known for its elaborate textiles. Immerse yourself in the art of weaving there. See the ancient Zapotec weaving methods that have been passed down through the generations to create colorful tapestries and rugs with symbolic designs.

3. Black Pottery (Barro Negro)

Take in San Bartolo Coyotepec's glossy elegance in their barro negro pottery. Explore the elaborate steps involved in shaping, polishing, and firing the clay to produce stunning black ceramics—a skill that is deeply rooted in Zapotec customs.

4. Oaxacan Ceramics

Discover the renowned Oaxaca pottery, which is produced using a variety of regional styles and techniques. Every piece of pottery, from the vivid green of Atzompa to the earthy hues of San Marcos Tlapazola, tells a tale of artistic expression and cultural identity.

5. Isthmus Textile Traditions

Explore the colorful textile traditions of the Tehuantepec Isthmus, where women wear rebozos and huipiles of vibrant colors that depict the rich cultural diversity of the Mixtec and Zapotec people.

Top Festivals and Celebrations

1. Día de los Muertos (Day of the Dead)

Take part in the vibrant celebration of Día de los Muertos, a poignant occasion to honor loved ones who have passed away. See colorful ofrendas (altars), deftly carved sugar skulls, and processions that light up the streets with a kaleidoscope of hues and feelings.

2. Guelaguetza (Oaxaca)

Take in the Oaxacan Guelaguetza festival's cultural extravaganza. As communities unite to celebrate their diversity, take in traditional dances, colorful costumes, and the sharing of local specialties.

3. Semana Santa, or Holy Week

Take in the solemn yet alluring Semana Santa customs, which commemorate the week of Holy Week that precedes Easter. All throughout Mexico, religious rites, elaborate reenactments, and processions take place, with each community adding its own special touch to the celebrations.

4. Noche de Rábanos (Night of the Radishes)

Enjoy the special Noche de Rábanos, which takes place on December 23. Admire the exquisite radish carvings in Oaxaca City's main square, which highlight the artistry and ingenuity of regional craftspeople.

5. Carnaval de Putla

Take part in the colorful parades, traditional dances, and upbeat music of this vibrant celebration, which takes place in February. Take in the festive atmosphere as the community joins together to celebrate this pre-Lenten celebration.

Must-See Colonial Architecture

1. Basilica of Our Lady of Guanajuato

Admire the magnificent neo-Gothic Basilica of Our Lady of Guanajuato, which serves as the city's emblem. The basilica, with its breathtaking spires and elaborate stained glass windows, is a symbol of Guanajuato's spiritual past.

2. Juárez Theater

Enter the opulence of Teatro Juárez, a stunning example of neoclassical and baroque architecture. The theater offers a captivating backdrop for artistic expression and cultural events thanks to its elaborate facade, imposing columns, and sumptuous interiors.

3. Guanajuato University

Discover the University of Guanajuato, an institution from the colonial era housed in an exquisite building with Baroque and Neoclassical architectural elements. Explore its courtyards, which are embellished with sculptures and fountains, to get a sense of the city's creative and intellectual spirit.

4. La Valenciana Church

Just outside of Guanajuato is the La Valenciana Church, a stunning example of Churrigueresque architecture. Admire the fine details of its facade, which highlights the Baroque splendor of the colonial era with intricate stonework and sculpted reliefs.

5. Jardín de la Unión

Take in the allure of this charming square encircled by buildings designed in the colonial style. Savor the atmosphere of the outdoor cafes, the famous kiosk, and the lively energy of this hub of activity.

6. Alley of the Kiss (Callejón del Beso)

Follow the Alley of the Kiss's winding streets as a romantic legend is framed by colonial architecture. Observe the balconies that are so close together that a couple could kiss across them, lending a romantic touch to Guanajuato's architectural story.

7. Hidalgo Market (Mercado Hidalgo)

Take a tour of this lively marketplace, which is housed in a historic structure with architecture influenced by Moorish design. Take in the vivid hues, scents, and tastes of regional goods as you take in the allure of this building from the colonial era.

8. Diego Rivera House-Museum

Enter Diego Rivera's childhood home, a colonial-style home that is currently used as a museum. Take in the building's architectural details and learn about the early years of the well-known Mexican muralist.

9. San Roque Church

Explore this colonial gem, which features Baroque elements on its facade. The interior of the church is decorated with elaborate altars, holy artwork, and a calm ambiance that captures the religious zeal of the colonists.

1. Cervantino International Festival

Take part in the internationally recognized Cervantino International Festival, a cultural extravaganza that elevates Guanajuato to a global platform. This festival highlights the variety of artistic expression with everything from dance and theater to visual arts and literature.

2. Festival Internacional de Jazz y Blues

Liven up your experience with jazz and blues at this event, where the soulful sounds of the genre fill the old streets. A unique musical atmosphere is created by the convergence of local and international musicians.

3. Festival Internacional de Cine Expresión en Corto

This event honors the craft of short filmmaking and is a chance to celebrate it. This film-related gathering unites enthusiasts, professionals in the field, and filmmakers to delve into the realm of short-form narrative.

4. Festival de las Almas

Explore the Festival de las Almas' creative and spiritual spheres. This festival delves into the intersections between creativity and spirituality through a harmonious celebration of music, dance, theater, and visual arts.

5. Festival Medieval de Guanajuato

Immerse yourself in a medieval extravaganza during this one-of-a-kind event that transports the city back in time. A unique immersive experience is provided by the convergence of artisans, minstrels, and knights who recreate the Middle Ages.

Exploring Underground Streets

1. Callejón del Beso (Alley of the Kiss)

Descend into the romantic legend of forbidden love that takes place in the subterranean passage beneath Callejón del Beso. By building a covert passageway through the center of Guanajuato, the hidden tunnel joins the two balconies connected to the tragic love tale.

2. Tunel del Tecolote (Owl's Tunnel)

Explore the enigmatic Tunel del Tecolote, a tunnel that runs beneath the city. Taking its name from the "Tunnel of the Owl," this underground path provides a distinctive viewpoint of Guanajuato's historic buildings.

3. Los Pastitos Tunnel

Discover the Los Pastitos Tunnel, an underground route that offers a direct route between the historic center of the city and the Mercado Hidalgo. Both residents and tourists can easily navigate the city beneath its busy streets thanks to this secret tunnel.

4. La Subterránea (The Subterranean)

Discover La Subterránea, an intricate system of tunnels that was formerly intended to control flooding but is now a fascinating subterranean route. Discover the underground passageways that link different areas of Guanajuato, providing a unique and atmospheric way to get around the city.

5. Plaza de la Paz Tunnel

Travel through the tunnel that connects the famous Basilica of Our Lady of Guanajuato to the Plaza de la Paz. The city's civic and religious sites have an air of mystery about them because of this underground route.

6. Mercado Hidalgo Underground Market

Explore the underground shopping destination located beneath the well-known market. Explore secret passageways filled with vendors selling a range of products, from regional crafts to

PUERTO VALLARTA AND THE
PACIFIC COAST

Best Beach Activities

1. Sunbathing and Relaxation

Relax on the golden sands of Los Muertos Beach or any
of the stunning beaches along Puerto Vallarta's coast.
Enjoy the ultimate in relaxation as you soak up the sun
and listen to the calming sound of the waves.

2. Water Sports

Enjoy a variety of water sports while diving into Banderas Bay's cool waters. For a thrilling experience against the breathtaking Pacific backdrop, try your hand at jet skiing, kayaking, or paddleboarding.

3. Snorkeling and Scuba Diving

Take a snorkel or scuba dive in the pristine waters to discover the rich underwater environment. The Marietas Islands offer the perfect backdrop for aquatic adventures because of their distinctive marine life and undiscovered beaches.

4. Beach Volleyball

Play a fun game of beach volleyball with nearby residents and other tourists. The ocean breeze and soft sands make for the ideal beachside setting for an exciting and fun match.

5. Parasailing

With parasailing, soar above the coast and enjoy breathtaking views from above. Savor the rush of taking off while being softly raised by a parachute, offering an unmatched view of Puerto Vallarta's splendor.

6. Sunset Cruises

Take a romantic Pacific Coast cruise as the sun sets. Sail the serene waters of Banderas Bay while taking in the breathtaking colors of the sunset, live music, and a delectable dinner.

7. Whale Watching

Take a whale-watching trip if you're there in the winter to see the magnificent humpback whales that travel to the warm waters of the Pacific. Witness the breathtaking spectacle of these kinds of giants breaching and having fun in the bay.

8. Beachfront Yoga

Yoga sessions on the beach can help you find balance and tranquility. Yoga sessions with the sound of the waves as your soothing backdrop are available at many resorts and beach clubs, making for a tranquil and restorative experience.

9. Beach Horseback Riding

Get in gear for an exciting beachside horseback riding excursion. As you stroll along the beaches and take in the breathtaking scenery of the coastal region, you can feel the soft cadence of the horse's walk.

Eco-Tourism

Take in the splendor of Puerto Vallarta and the Pacific Coast while resolving to support ecotourism and sustainable travel. Explore eco-friendly projects and establish a connection with nature along the Pacific coast.

1. Puerto Vallarta Botanical Gardens

Let yourself get lost in the lush vegetation of this garden. The gardens, which are devoted to conservation and education, offer a peaceful haven for those who enjoy the outdoors. They feature a varied assortment of native plants and orchids.

2. Sea Turtle Conservation

Get involved in neighborhood projects to support efforts to conserve sea turtles. Numerous organizations located along the Pacific Coast are committed to safeguarding the nesting sites and perpetuating the existence of these amazing animals.

3. Mangrove Exploration

Take an eco-friendly boat tour to learn about the mangroves' important ecosystems. These excursions stress the value of protecting these coastal habitats while also providing a distinctive viewpoint on the complex mangrove ecosystems.

4. Eco-Friendly Excursions

Choose environmentally friendly trips that put an emphasis on ethical travel methods. Select activities that reduce the ecological footprint and raise environmental awareness, such as bird-watching tours and guided nature hikes.

5. Sayulita's Eco-Surf Scene

Take a look at Sayulita's eco-surf scene, where sustainability is given priority by surf schools and operators. Discover how to surf responsibly and support campaigns that save the ocean by learning to ride the waves.

1. Ceviche Varieties

Explore the cool world of ceviche, a recipe that blends citrusy flavors with fresh seafood. Try the shrimp, fish, or mixed seafood ceviche varieties; they're all full of flavorful, tangy goodness.

2. Aguachile

This dish, which resembles ceviche but has a fiery kick, is flavorful and spicy. For those who enjoy a little heat, shrimp marinated in a broth infused with chilies makes for a delicious culinary experience.

3. Grilled Fish Tacos

Savor the ease of preparation and flawless flavor of these tacos. Warm tortillas are stuffed with perfectly cooked, freshly caught fish that has been grilled. Crisp cabbage, pico de gallo, and a creamy sauce drizzle are served on top.

4. Shrimp Tostadas

Treat yourself to shrimp tostadas, where colorful salsas, crisp tortillas, and succulent shrimp make the ideal combination. Every bite of this dish demonstrates the harmony of flavors and textures.

5. Mariscada

Savor the delectable mariscada, a seafood medley comprising a variety of marine delicacies. A rich and flavorful celebration of the sea, mariscada offers a variety of seafood, from clams and mussels to shrimp and octopus.

6. Seafood Empanadas

Savor the mouthwatering goodness of these savory empanadas, which are filled with delectable seafood. The pastry is flaky. These portable sweets are ideal for an easy and filling beachside snack.

7. Pescado Zarandeado

Sample the grilled and marinated fish dish known as pescado zarandeado. This dish, which is made with a combination of herbs and spices, exemplifies the richness and simplicity of Pacific Coast cooking.

8. Lobster with Butter and Garlic

Savor the elegance of lobster cooked in garlic butter. This luscious dish brings out the sweet and tender characteristics of lobster, enhanced by the rich and fragrant flavors of butter infused with garlic.

9. Molcajete with Seafood

Enjoy a communal dish called seafood molcajete, which is served in a volcanic stone mortar. This filling and aromatic dish is a veritable culinary showpiece, piled high with shrimp, fish, and other delectable seafood.

CHIAPAS

Exploring Natural Wonders

1. Montebello Lakes National Park

Take in the kaleidoscope beauty of Montebello Lakes, where the immaculate waters reflect a rainbow of colors. Discover the many lakes in the park, each with a distinct shade, encircled by verdant forests and picturesque paths.

2. Agua Azul Waterfalls

The Agua Azul Waterfalls are a stunning sequence of waterfalls with turquoise-hued pools. Take in the cascading beauty of these natural wonders. The rich greenery and vivid blue waters combine to create a captivating sight that beckons you to enjoy the beauty of nature.

3. Sumidero Canyon

Take a cruise through the Grijalva River's sculpted tall cliffs at Sumidero Canyon. Marvel at the striking rock formations, see a variety of wildlife and let the canyon's majestic presence enthrall you as it reveals the force of nature.

4. El Chiflón Waterfalls

Discover El Chiflón Waterfalls by hiking through verdant landscapes. Here, pure water cascades through a series of falls encircled by vivid greenery. For those who love the outdoors, the calm ambiance and cool mist make it a sanctuary.

5. Lacandón Jungle

Go deep into this enormous rainforest, which is brimming with wildlife. Discover historic Mayan ruins tucked away amid lush vegetation and take in the unadulterated splendor of one of Mexico's most important natural reserves.

6. Chiapas Amber Route

Discover the geological marvel of amber by traveling along the Chiapas Amber Route. Discover the amber deposits of the Simojovel region and the skillful craftsmanship that goes into turning this age-old resin into jewelry.

7. La Venta Archaeological Park

Explore the artistic and cultural accomplishments of the mysterious Olmec civilization at La Venta Archaeological Park, where enormous stone heads and prehistoric buildings showcase their achievements. The park is evidence of the rich archaeological history of the area.

8. Canyon del Sumidero

Take in the grandeur of this natural wonder from high vantage points as you explore Canyon del Sumidero. The Grijalva River, the canyon's steep walls, and the rich vegetation combine to create a mesmerizing scene that demonstrates the Earth's skill as a sculptor.

9. Grutas de Rancho Nuevo

Venture into the network of caverns here to discover the underground splendor of stalactites and stalagmites. Explore lit rooms and be in awe of the geological treasures hidden beneath Chiapas' surface.

10. Volcán Tacaná

Admire the magnificence of Volcán Tacaná, a massive stratovolcano close to the Guatemalan border. Encircled by verdant forests, the volcano presents expansive vistas and a chance to observe the geological dynamics that mold the area.

Indigenous Communities to Visit

Take a cultural tour of Chiapas and discover the diverse array of indigenous communities that have influenced the area's rich history.

1. Zinacantán

Get to know the Tzotzil Maya people of Zinacantán, who are renowned for their vibrant textile customs and spiritual ceremonies. See how intricate designs and vivid

73

colors are brought to life on traditional clothing through the weaving process.

2. San Juan Chamula

At San Juan Chamula, take part in the mysterious rites of the Tzeltal Maya. Visit the local church to witness the manifestation of a unique ceremony that combines Catholicism with ancient beliefs. Take in the lively markets and learn about this community's unique cultural identity.

3. Lacandón People

Make contact with the indigenous Lacandón people who live in the Lacandón Jungle. Discover the sustainable practices and strong spiritual ties to the natural world that define their traditional way of life.

4. Tenejapa

Discover the customs of the Tzeltal Maya in Tenejapa, where ornate garments, dexterous needlework, and ritualistic activities showcase the community's cultural pride. Interact with the community during celebrations to learn about their artistic expressions.

5. Tsotsil Maya in San Cristóbal de las Casas

Discover this community in San Cristóbal de las Casas, where you can find handcrafted goods and textiles at traditional markets. See how the modern dynamics of this thriving highland town coexist with centuries-old customs.

6. Tojolabal People

Discover the traditions of the Tojolabal people, an aboriginal people group with a strong agricultural history. Discover their farming methods, customs, and the value of community life in maintaining their cultural identity.

7. Tzeltal Maya in Amatenango del Valle

Take a trip to Amatenango del Valle, a town well-known for its customs pertaining to the creation of pottery. Interact with Tzeltal Maya artists as they create works of art in clay that represent both secular and sacred themes.

8. Zoque People

Make contact with the indigenous Zoque people who live in Chiapas' lowlands. Discover their unique traditions, which include dances and ceremonies honoring their ties to the land.

1. White-Water Rafting on the Grijalva River

Get ready for the thrilling Grijalva River rapids as you make your way through the breathtaking Sumidero Canyon. With towering cliffs and lush greenery as a backdrop, white-water rafting provides an exhilarating experience.

2. Jungle Zip-Lining in Palenque

Take a zip-lining adventure through the jungle's treetops. Savor the exhilaration of effortlessly navigating through the dense foliage, catching glimpses of historic ruins beneath you, and taking in Chiapas' breathtaking natural splendor.

3. Mountain Biking in the Lacandón Jungle

Get ready for an exciting off-road cycling experience on the difficult paths found in the Lacandón Jungle. Experience the varied flora and fauna that make this jungle a mountain biker's dream come true as you weave through thick vegetation, cross rivers, and discover.

4. Caving in Grutas de Rancho Nuevo

Experience the amazing caving world of Grutas de Rancho Nuevo by venturing into its underground realm. Discover lit rooms, squeeze through tight spaces, and take in the elaborate formations that adorn these hidden caverns.

5. Hiking to El Chiflón Waterfalls

Take a picturesque hike through verdant meadows and unspoiled nature paths to reach El Chiflón Waterfalls. Hikers are rewarded with a refreshing and breathtaking view of the cascading waterfalls at the end of their journey.

6. Rock Climbing in the Chiapas Highlands

Take on rock climbing adventures to overcome the region's vertical challenges. Climb jagged cliffs encircled by expansive vistas, putting your abilities to the test against this highland region's rough terrain.

7. Cave Rafting in Sumidero Canyon

Cavern rafting in Sumidero Canyon is an exciting way to explore caves. Experience the excitement of an underground adventure as you navigate through underground river passageways, finding secret chambers along the way.

8. Paragliding Over Chiapas Landscapes

Take a paragliding adventure to soar above the landscapes of Chiapas like a bird. Take in breathtaking aerial views of mountains, jungles, and historic sites while you soar through the skies.

9. Horseback Riding in Zinacantán

Get ready for an exciting horseback ride through Zinacantán's stunning scenery. Discover historic towns, undulating terrain, and cultural sites while establishing a connection with the local way of life.

10. Cave Diving in Cenotes

Explore Chiapas's secret labyrinth by going cave diving in cenotes. Discover the captivating formations and pristine waters that make Chiapas a haven for cave diving enthusiasts as you explore underwater cave systems.

MONTERREY AND NORTHERN MEXICO

Modern Urban Life

Discover the dynamic pulse of Monterrey, a city where innovation and modernity meet against the stunning backdrop of the mountains. Take a deep dive into Monterrey's vibrant, modern urban life:

1. Monterrey's Skyline

Take in the city's striking skyline, which is adorned with tall skyscrapers that showcase its inventiveness and economic might. Discover how contemporary architecture creates a dynamic visual spectacle by reshaping the urban environment.

2. Financial and Business Districts

Explore Monterrey's thriving financial and business districts, which are the main engines of the region's economy in Northern Mexico. Discover cutting-edge financial institutions, contemporary office buildings, and the vibrant energy of a city at the forefront of innovation.

3. Macroplaza: The City's Heart

Take a leisurely stroll around Macroplaza, the large central square that forms Monterrey's center. Admire well-known sites, such as the Faro del Comercio, and take in the harmony of modern architecture, historical sites, and green areas.

4. Paseo Santa Lucía: Urban Oasis

Stroll along the picturesque canal that winds through the city, Paseo Santa Lucía, an urban oasis. Take a leisurely boat ride and enjoy how Monterrey's modern urban design incorporates nature into the cityscape.

5. Technological and Cultural Institutions

Learn about the institutions that support Monterrey's technological and cultural vibrancy. See the museums, cultural institutions, and the Monterrey Institute of Technology and Higher Education (ITESM) to witness the city's dedication to learning and advancement.

6. Contemporary Art and Design Scene

Take in the galleries, street art, and cutting-edge installations that define Monterrey's modern art and design scene. See how regional artists contribute to the cultural fabric of the city, which captures the essence of contemporary urban living.

7. Modern Shopping and Entertainment Centers

Take advantage of contemporary shopping and entertainment options at the posh malls and entertainment hubs in Monterrey. Explore an abundance of global and regional brands, eat at hip restaurants, and take in cultural events that embody Monterrey's sophisticated way of life.

8. Technological Innovation Hubs

Find out how Monterrey promotes entrepreneurship and technological advancements by acting as a hub for technological innovation. See the innovation hubs, co-working spaces, and startup incubators that support the vibrant business scene in the city.

9. Sustainable Urban Development

Discover Monterrey's dedication to environmentally friendly city planning. Explore environmentally conscious projects, green areas, and sustainable architecture that showcase the city's commitment to striking a balance between contemporary living and environmental awareness.

10. Entertainment and Nightlife Districts

Relax in the trendy bars, clubs, and entertainment venues that come to life after dusk in Monterrey's entertainment districts and vibrant nightlife. Discover the vibrant environment and social scene that characterize Monterrey's nightlife.

Top Outdoor Adventures

1. Rock Climbing in Potrero Chico

Take on the imposing limestone cliffs of Potrero Chico, a popular spot for rock climbing worldwide. The sheer cliffs and amazing views provide an amazing ascent for any level of climber, experienced or not.

2. Parque Chipinque: Hiking Paradise

Follow the network of trails through verdant forests and sweeping vistas as you explore Parque Chipinque, a hiking paradise. For a breathtaking view of Monterrey and the surrounding mountains, hike to the summit.

3. La Huasteca Horseback Riding

Mount up for an exciting horseback riding excursion in La Huasteca, a natural park outside of Monterrey. Travel by horseback through a variety of environments, from craggy canyons to peaceful riverbank paths, and take in the splendor of Northern Mexico.

4. Sierra Madre Oriente: Mountain Bike Extravaganza

In the mountain range that envelops Monterrey, take off on an incredible mountain biking adventure. Explore difficult paths, ski down exhilarating hills, and experience the exhilaration of off-road cycling.

5. Caving in Grutas de García: Underground Exploration

Take a plunge into caving adventures in Grutas de García to explore below ground. Explore underground passageways decorated with breathtaking formations and take in the distinct beauty of these limestone caverns.

6. La Estanzuela: Zip-lining and Canopy Tours

In this ecological park outside of Monterrey, take in the exhilaration of zip-lining and canopy tours. Take in the expansive views of the surrounding landscape as you soar through the treetops.

7. Cola de Caballo: Waterfall Rappelling

At the breathtaking waterfall in the Cumbres de Monterrey National Park, Cola de Caballo is a thrilling waterfall rappelling experience. Climb down beside the gushing water for a thrilling descent.

8. Santiago: Kayaking on Presa de la Boca

Take a kayaking adventure through the calm waters of Presa de la Boca in Santiago. Savor the peace and quiet of the reservoir while it is surrounded by a profusion of vegetation and the untamed splendor of the Northern Mexican terrain.

9. Monterrey Hot Air Ballooning

Soar through the skies while hot air ballooning over the city. Take in the striking mountains and expansive cityscape from an unusual and tranquil vantage point as you float above the city and its environs.

10. La Huasteca Climbing Garden: Sport Climbing Paradise

Explore the La Huasteca Climbing Garden, a space set aside for sport climbing, and let your climbing abilities run wild. Climbers can enjoy the challenge in front of breathtaking scenery, with a range of routes accommodating varying skill levels.

OFF-THE-BEATEN-PATH

ADVENTURES

Top Hidden Gems to Discover

1. Las Coloradas

Experience the ethereal splendor of Las Coloradas, where vivid pink lakes envelop the landscape. The high concentration of salt and microorganisms in this hidden gem of the Yucatán Peninsula creates a breathtaking visual spectacle.

2. Cuetzalan

Climb to the charming town of Cuetzalan, which is tucked away in the Sierra Norte's clouds. Cuetzalan, with its traditional markets, cobblestone streets, and the enigmatic Yohualichan archaeological site, is a pueblo mágico (magic town) that offers a fusion of charm and culture.

3. Marieta Islands

Discover the Marieta Islands, where the renowned Hidden Beach is located. Reachable by boat, this private island boasts a hidden beach within a collapsed volcanic crater, encircled by pristine waters and an abundance of colorful marine life.

4. Cenote Ik Kil

Explore the depths of Cenote Ik Kil, a captivating sinkhole close to Chichen Itza that is encircled by lush jungle. Enjoy a revitalizing swim in its emerald-green waters or awe at the natural beauty and cascading vines that make this hidden oasis.

5. Xilitla

Take in the bizarre sculptures of eccentric artist Edward James at Xilitla's Las Pozas. Explore this whimsical art installation, hidden staircases, and towering structures that make up this jungle wonderland.

6. Isla Espíritu Santo

Set sail for Isla Espíritu Santo, an unspoiled piece of paradise in the Sea of Cortez. This UNESCO World Heritage site offers chances to see playful sea lions and a variety of marine life, along with immaculate beaches and turquoise waters.

7. Bernal's Monolith

In the quaint town of Bernal, marvel at the third-largest monolith in the world. Rising dramatically from the landscape, Peña de Bernal is a sacred rock that offers panoramic views and a sense of spiritual significance.

8. Coba

Explore the historic Maya city of Coba, which is tucked away in a jungle on the Yucatán Peninsula. Discover hidden pyramids while cycling through the archaeological site, such as the imposing Nohoch Mul, which offers a singular and immersive exploration experience.

9. Grutas de Cacahuamilpa

Go underground and explore one of the world's largest cave systems, Grutas de Cacahuamilpa. Discover enormous rooms filled with stalactites and stalagmites that create a fascinating subterranean world.

10. Hidalgo's English Influence at Real del Monte

Enter the mining town of Real del Monte, renowned for its mouthwatering pastes (savory pastries) and English architectural influence. Discover this undiscovered gem by meandering through cobblestone streets, stopping by the English Cemetery, and relishing the distinctive fusion of cultures.

1. San Juan Chamula, Chiapas

Take in the distinctive customs of San Juan Chamula, home to a thriving Tzotzil Maya community. Explore the bustling local market and observe historic rites in the church, which is decorated with a mix of Catholicism and traditional beliefs.

2. Candelaria, Campeche

Visit Candelaria, a colonial gem in Campeche, to travel back in time. Explore the colorful houses lining the cobblestone streets, pay a visit to the ancient San Román church, and feel the genuine coziness of this remote village.

3. Batopilas, Chihuahua

Tucked away in the Copper Canyon area, discover the undiscovered gem of Batopilas. Reachable via a meandering road, this isolated community provides an insight into the untamed splendor of the canyon, the history of silver mining, and the diverse cultural heritage of the Tarahumara people.

4. Huautla de Jiménez, Oaxaca

Head into the Oaxaca mountains to arrive at Huautla de Jiménez, a village renowned for its hallucinogenic mushroom rituals and mystical traditions. Explore the surrounding natural beauties and interact with the Mazatec culture of this isolated community.

5. Yaxchilán, Chiapas

Yaxchilán is an ancient Maya city tucked away in the heart of the Chiapas jungle. To get there, navigate the Usumacinta River. Experience the link to the past Maya civilization as you explore this beautifully preserved archaeological site, renowned for its exquisitely carved stelae and breathtaking architecture.

6. Tlaxcala de Xicohténcatl, Tlaxcala

Take in the diversity of culture in one of Mexico's smallest states, Tlaxcala de Xicohténcatl. This quaint town has indigenous customs, colonial architecture, and a welcoming community that extends a warm welcome to guests.

7. Yelapa, Jalisco

Get away to Yelapa, a seaside village that can only be reached by boat from Puerto Vallarta. Relax on immaculate beaches, take in the views of the lush jungle, and take in the laid-back vibe of this remote paradise.

8. Cuetzalan del Progreso, Puebla

Climb to the cloud-covered peaks of Cuetzalan del Progreso, a magical town known for its verdant surroundings and native culture. Discover the town's historic center, pay a visit to the Tosepan Kali community project, and take in customary rituals honoring the area's cultural legacy.

9. Santa María del Tule, Oaxaca

Visit Santa María del Tule, the location of El Árbol del Tule, the widest tree in the world, and see the ancient Montezuma cypress. With its centuries-old customs, this village provides a tranquil environment to enjoy the natural world and get a sense of Oaxacan culture.

10. Malinalco, State of Mexico

Discover the charm and history of Malinalco, a pre-Hispanic village. Explore the Ex-Convento Agustino, admire the archaeological site, and meander through the streets lined with adobe houses to get a sense of this classic Mexican village.

Top Unique Experiences

1. Mezcal Tasting in Oaxaca

In the mezcal-producing region of Oaxaca, immerse yourself in the rich tradition of mezcal. Experience the complex flavors of this artisanal spirit, learn about the craft of mezcal production by visiting nearby palenques (distilleries), speaking with maestros mezcaleros, and tasting the product.

2. Lucha Libre Spectacle in Mexico City

Discover the thrilling world of Lucha Libre, the renowned professional wrestling style from Mexico. Take in a live match in Mexico City, where mask-wearing luchadores display their theatrical performances, colorful costumes, and acrobatic prowess in an unforgettable cultural spectacle.

3. Day of the Dead Celebration in Patzcuaro

See the colorful and emotional Dia de los Muertos (Day of the Dead) celebrations in the enchanted town of Patzcuaro. Take part in processions led by candlelight, pay respects to the deceased with customary offerings, music, and dance, and visit cemeteries decked with marigolds.

4. Hot Air Balloon Ride over Teotihuacan

Take in the amazing aerial view as you soar above the historic pyramids of Teotihuacan in a hot air balloon. Savor the grandeur of this historical marvel and its ethereal surrounds as the sun rises over the Pyramid of the Sun and the Pyramid of the Moon.

5. Volcano Boarding in Cerro Negro

On the slopes of Cerro Negro in Nicaragua, go volcano boarding for an exhilarating adventure. Adventure seekers will have a thrilling and unforgettable experience descending the ash-covered slopes of this active volcano while strapped onto a board.

6. Floating Mariachis in Xochimilco

Take a colorful trajinera (traditional boat) ride through the charming canals of Xochimilco while listening to mariachi music. Savor the upbeat music and lively atmosphere, and consider dancing on the boat to really get into the holiday spirit.

7. Mystic Temazcal Ceremony

Use a traditional Temazcal ceremony to cleanse your body and soul. This age-old Aztec sweat lodge ritual offers a restorative and immersive experience in harmony with Mexican customs. It includes herbal steam, traditional chants, and spiritual guidance.

8. Sumidero Canyon Boat Tour

Take a boat tour through Chiapas' Sumidero Canyon and see the lush scenery and dramatic cliffs. Discover wildlife, take in the breathtaking vistas of towering rock formations, and lose yourself in this breathtaking canyon's natural beauty.

9. Cenote Diving on the Yucatán Peninsula

For a one-of-a-kind diving experience, descend into the glistening clear cenotes on the peninsula. Discover hidden chambers, underwater cave systems, and stalactite formations in these revered natural sinkholes.

10. Snorkeling with whale sharks in Holbox

Go whale shark snorkeling in the waters off Isla Holbox and swim with these gentle giants. It is an amazing and ethereal experience to see these magnificent animals in their natural environment.

MULTILINGUAL MEXICO: LANGUAGES AND CUSTOMS

Indigenous Languages

1. Nahuatl:

Learn Nahuatl, the language used by communities in central Mexico, and lose yourself in the world of the Aztecs. Learn about its complex symbolism and poetic expressions, which preserve the heritage of one of the most significant Mesoamerican civilizations.

2. Maya Languages

Visit the southern regions of Mexico and the Yucatán Peninsula to learn about the Yucatec, Q'eqchi', and K'iche' Maya languages. These languages have a linguistic heritage that spans thousands of years, connecting them to the ancient Mayan civilization.

3. Zapotec

Discover the language of the Zapotec people who live in Oaxaca's valleys and mountains. Zapotec people reflect the cultural diversity of the region through their distinctive dialects. Discover the subtle cultural nuances and rich oral traditions that are ingrained in Zapotec communication.

4. Mixtec

Explore the communities that speak Mixtec, mainly in Puebla, Guerrero, and Oaxaca. The stories of a vibrant pre-Columbian Mesoamerican civilization are preserved in the Tonal Variations of the Mixtec Language.

5. Otomi

Encounter the language of the Otomi people, who live in central Mexico. Otomi, one of the most extensively spoken indigenous languages, reflects the Otomi people's strong ties to the land by carrying the stories, myths, and wisdom of the people.

Spanish Expressions

1. ¡A Huevo!

This phrase, which literally translates as "to the egg," is used to express vehement agreement or affirmation. It gives your remarks a little more vigor and emphasis. ¡Que lindo es! (Unquestionably, yes!)

2. Estar en las Nubes

This expression, which means "to be in the clouds," is used to characterize someone who is not paying attention or is daydreaming. It's a lighthearted way of letting someone know when their thoughts are straying.

3. Más Vale Tarde Que Nunca

"Better Late Than Never." This classic saying highlights how important it is to finish what needs to be done or keep your word, even if it's a little bit late. A gracious method to acknowledge lateness.

4. Meter la Pata

"To put your foot in it." When someone says or does something improper or embarrassing, this idiom is used. It's a lighthearted method of admitting a social faux pas.

5. Ser pan comido

This expression, which literally translates as "to be eaten bread," indicates that something is simple or straightforward to accomplish. Apply it to tasks that are simple or easy.

6. Echar Agua al Mar

This expression, which means "to throw water into the sea," is used to characterize an ineffective or senseless deed. It communicates the idea of taking action without any true consequence or impact.

7. No Hay Mal Que por Bien No Venga

"Every cloud has a silver lining." This upbeat statement highlights the notion that even in trying circumstances, good things might come of them.

8. Dar en el Clavo

This expression, which means "to hit the nail on the head," is used when someone says something precise or factual. It accepts that a statement is accurate.

9. Tirar la Casa por la Ventana:

"To throw the house out the window." This expression is used when someone is going all out for a celebration or event or is spending extravagantly. It implies a readiness to spend everything.

TRANSPORTATION AND GETTING AROUND

1. Metro Systems

Take in the effectiveness of Mexico's metro systems, which are especially noteworthy in busy cities like Mexico City. Discover how to use the vast network of lines that connects you to important neighborhoods and attractions.

2. Bus Networks

Investigate the vast bus networks that intersect both rural and urban environments. Learn how buses connect towns and cities all over the nation as an affordable and easily accessible mode of transportation.

3. Suburban Trains

Savor the ease of suburban trains as they link surrounding areas with urban centers. These trains provide a pleasant means of traveling to areas outside of cities and offer beautiful scenery as you go.

4. Tram Systems

Explore cities that have tram systems—a quaint and nostalgic way to get around. Trams wind through neighborhoods with historical significance, letting you experience the local flavor while getting where you're going.

5. Colectivos and Shared Taxis

Welcome the shared spirit of passengers being transported along predetermined routes in colectivos, shared vans, or taxis. Colectivos are a social and economic option that is perfect for short-distance travel.

6. EcoBici and Bike-Sharing Programs

Use bike-sharing services like EcoBici to pedal through urban environments. Find out how these programs encourage environmentally friendly transportation so you can see cities at your own speed.

7. Accessibility Features

Discover how Mexico's public transportation has been incorporated with accessibility features. The system makes an effort to accommodate all passengers, offering amenities like elevators and ramps as well as special places for those with disabilities.

8. Ticketing and Payment Systems

Handle payment and ticketing systems with ease. Discover how to make your experience using public transit more efficient by taking advantage of reloadable cards, smartphone apps, and cash payments.

9. Customs and Social Protocols

Recognize the customs and etiquette related to using public transit. These conventions, which range from providing seats to elderly travelers to honoring quiet areas, improve everyone's experience.

10. Safety Tips

Put your safety first when taking public transit. To guarantee a safe and comfortable travel, familiarize yourself with emergency exits, pay attention to your surroundings, and abide by the rules.

Renting a Car

1. Pros and Cons of Renting a Car:

Before taking a road trip, weigh the benefits and factors. Take advantage of the freedom to visit places off the beaten path, but drive carefully and respectfully of the laws of the road, traffic patterns, and driving customs.

2. Rental Agencies

Look through the many rental companies that have a range of cars to choose from for your trip. Select a trustworthy company with clear terms when selecting a vehicle, whether it's a sturdy SUV for off-road excursions or a tiny car for city exploration.

3. Documentation Requirements

Make sure everything is ready for the rental process so that it goes smoothly. Make sure you have an up-to-date driver's license, a credit card for the security deposit, and proof of identity, like a passport, available for verification.

4. Road Conditions and Safety

Learn about the safety regulations and state of the roads. Mexico's varied geography makes for picturesque driving, but it's better to know the topography, the weather, and any potential dangers before you take a car.

5. Toll Roads and Payment

Accept the expediency of Mexico's toll roads for a more rapid and seamless travel experience. Carry cash for transactions and be ready to pay tolls. Toll collections go toward keeping roads in good condition.

6. Apps for GPS and Navigation

Arm yourself with trustworthy navigational aids. Accurate navigation, whether through a GPS device or smartphone apps, guarantees that you arrive at your destinations without needless detours.

7. Fueling Up

Easily navigate gas stations. There are lots of gas stations, and you usually pay after you fill up. Learn about local fueling customs, including full-service options.

8. Parking in Urban Centers

Take control of city centers with well-planned parking. Recognize local laws and payment methods before parking on designated lots or the street to prevent needless fines.

9. Returning the Rental Car:

Follow the instructions provided by the rental agency to guarantee a simple return procedure. Before ending your rental, make sure there are no damages, return the vehicle with a full tank of gas, and pay any outstanding balances.

Best Scenic Train Routes

1. Copper Canyon Railway

Take the Copper Canyon Railway for an incredible journey through the Sierra Madre Occidental. This fascinating experience allows you to see the Tarahumara culture, traverse tall bridges, and navigate rough canyons.

2. Tequila Express

Savor the tastes of tequila, the well-known spirit of Mexico, on board the Tequila Express. This picturesque train ride passes through Jalisco's agave fields, providing breathtaking vistas of the terrain that inspires this well-known drink.

3. Chepe Express

As it winds through the Copper Canyon, take in the luxury of the Chepe Express. Admire expansive vistas, savor fine dining, and unwind in comfort as you travel through this magnificent area.

4. Ferrocarril Interoceánico

Discover the historical significance of the railway known as the Ferrocarril Interoceánico, which once linked the Gulf of Mexico and the Pacific Ocean. The remaining portions of this route provide a window into the history of Mexico.

5. Pacifico Railroad

This railroad, which links the states of Chihuahua and Sinaloa, allows you to travel around the Pacific coast. Travel this scenic route and take in the views of the coast, verdant landscapes, and quaint towns.

ACCOMMODATION OPTIONS

Top Luxury Resorts

1. Rosewood Mayakoba, Riviera Maya

Situated amidst verdant jungle and immaculate beaches, Rosewood Mayakoba provides secluded suites and villas featuring plunge pools along the Riviera Maya. Enjoy sumptuous meals, spa services, and luxurious surroundings.

2. Las Ventanas al Paraíso, Los Cabos

With its beachfront suites and butler service to match, Las Ventanas al Paraíso, which overlooks the Sea of Cortez's azure waters, captivates guests. Savor top-notch facilities and breathtaking views of the sea and desert.

3. Imanta Resorts Punta de Mita, Punta de Mita

This resort offers oceanfront casas that seamlessly blend in with the surrounding natural environment. Come experience exclusivity at Punta de Mita, Nayarit. An exclusive beach, fine dining, and private infinity pools combine to create a luxurious and intimate atmosphere.

4. One&Only Palmilla in Los Cabos, Baja California Sur

With a reputation for excellence, One&Only Palmilla provides gorgeous villas and suites with views of the Sea of Cortez. In this renowned luxury resort, take advantage of award-winning spa treatments, Michelin-starred dining, and impeccable service.

5. Hotel Esencia, Xpu-Ha, Quintana Roo

Constructed on the site of a former private estate, Hotel Esencia offers opulence amid a tranquil tropical environment. Enjoy gourmet dining, spa treatments that will revitalize you, and suites right on the beach.

6. Chablé Resort & Spa, Chocholá, Yucatán

Indulge in the luxurious, wellness-focused atmosphere of Chablé Resort & Spa. This resort, housed in a renovated hacienda, features private villas, an excellent spa, and dining options that celebrate the flavors of Yucatán.

7. St. Regis Punta Mita Resort, Punta de Mita, Nayarit

At the St. Regis Punta Mita Resort, which offers opulent lodging with views of the ocean, revel in coastal elegance. Take advantage of fine dining, butler service, and golf courses designed by Jack Nicklaus.

8. Four Seasons Resort Costa Palmas, Los Cabos, Baja California Sur

Tucked away along the Sea of Cortez, Four Seasons Resort Costa Palmas offers tranquility. This beachside sanctuary is defined by tasteful villas, a private marina, and a Robert Trent Jones II golf course.

9. Grand Velas Riviera Maya, Playa del Carmen

Indulge in luxury at this all-inclusive resort featuring roomy suites, fine dining, and an award-winning spa. The resort combines an emphasis on sustainability with luxury.

10. NIZUC Resort & Spa, Cancún

Located on a private peninsula, this modern luxury resort has Mayan influences. Savor gourmet meals, roomy suites, and the peace of azure waters and verdant surroundings.

Boutique Hotels

1. Condesa DF, Mexico City

At Condesa DF, get fully immersed in the bustling La Condesa neighborhood. This boutique hotel offers chic accommodations, a rooftop terrace, and easy access to local attractions all while fusing modern and colonial architectural elements.

2. Casa Fayette, Guadalajara, Jalisco

Experience modern elegance at Casa Fayette. Modern architecture, a rooftop pool, and attentive service encapsulate Mexico's creative spirit.

3. L'átel at Doce18 Concept House, San Miguel de Allende, Guanajuato

At L'átel in San Miguel de Allende, you can enjoy luxury in a historically significant setting. This boutique hotel, housed within Doce18 Concept House, creates a distinctive and fashionable retreat by fusing modern conveniences with colonial charm.

4. Hotel Matilda, San Miguel de Allende, Guanajuato:

Revel in modern luxury at Hotel Matilda, a renowned hotel with art-inspired decor and high-end accommodations. The modern design of this boutique hotel blends in perfectly with the cultural legacy of San Miguel de Allende.

5. Coqui Coqui Valladolid, Valladolid, Yucatán

Take a break at the boutique hotel in the center of Yucatán, Coqui Coqui Valladolid. This charming hideaway offers a peaceful haven in the middle of history by fusing individualized service with Mayan-inspired architecture.

6. Dôce 18 Concept House, San Miguel de Allende

Visit Dôce 18 Concept House to discover how art, culture, and hospitality converge. This distinctive boutique hotel offers specially created suites, artisan stores, and a carefully chosen menu.

Budget-Friendly Stays

1. Hostel Mundo Joven Catedral, Mexico City, CDMX

Stay at Hostel Mundo Joven Catedral to fully immerse yourself in the city's center. With affordable private and dorm room options available at this conveniently located hostel, you can explore the bustling capital on a tight budget.

2. Selina Playa del Carmen Downtown, Quintana Roo

At Selina Downtown, you can take in the carefree atmosphere of Playa del Carmen, Quintana Roo. This reasonably priced lodging is perfect for travelers on a tight budget because it provides a variety of options, including private rooms and shared dorms.

3. Hostel Che Tulum - Tulum, Quintana Roo

At Hostel Che, you can experience the free-spirited vibe of Tulum. Offering communal areas and dormitory beds at a reasonable price, it offers an economical starting point for discovering the Riviera Maya's beaches, cenotes, and Mayan ruins.

4. Casa Pepe, Guanajuato

Visit Casa Pepe to experience the allure of Guanajuato without going over budget. From this affordable guesthouse, you can walk to the city's historic sites while enjoying comfortable accommodations in a convenient location.

5. Hostel Ka'beh, Mérida, Yucatán

Stay at Hostel Ka'beh to fully immerse yourself in Mérida, the cultural center of Yucatán. This inexpensive hostel is a great option for travelers on a tight budget who want to explore the area because it offers a variety of accommodations and a friendly atmosphere.

6. Hostal Azul Cielo, Puerto Vallarta, Jalisco

Stay at Hostal Azul Cielo to take in the lively charm of Puerto Vallarta. For those on a tight budget who want to explore the beaches and nightlife, this hostel offers both private rooms and dorm beds.

7. Hostal Chocolate, Oaxaca City, Oaxaca

Spend a night at Hostal Chocolate to experience the city's rich cultural diversity. Combining private and dorm accommodations, this inexpensive hostel makes for a cozy and cost-effective home base.

PRACTICAL TIPS FOR A SMOOTH STAY

Currency and Money Matters

1. Mexican Peso (MXN)

The Mexican Peso (MXN) is the official currency of Mexico. Get acquainted with the various coin and bill denominations, including centavos.

2. Currency Exchange

Get competitive rates when exchanging currencies at licensed currency exchange offices (casas de cambio). Don't exchange money at hotels or airports where the exchange rates might be worse.

3. ATMs

For convenience, use ATMs to withdraw pesos. If you want safe transactions, only use ATMs connected to reliable banks. To prevent any problems, be mindful of withdrawal fees and let your bank know when you will be traveling.

4. Credit and Debit Cards

In cities and popular tourist locations, major credit and debit cards are commonly accepted. In order to avoid any unforeseen card problems, let your bank know about your travel schedule. For smaller businesses, always have some cash on you.

5. Tipping Culture

Mexico has a tipping culture. A standard tip in restaurants is between 10% and 15%. For services such as tour guides, hotel staff, and taxis, leave small tips. Verify whether your bill includes a service charge.

6. Bargaining and Cash Payments

Cash is frequently preferred in marketplaces and smaller businesses. Develop your negotiating abilities, particularly in marketplaces, but do it with courtesy. Small bills can come in handy for these kinds of transactions.

7. Safety Measures

Use caution when handling your cash and possessions. Keep valuables secure in a pouch or money belt, and stay away from flaunting big sums of cash in public. Copies of crucial documents should be stored somewhere different.

8. Setting a Travel Budget:

Make sure to budget for lodging, food, travel, and entertainment in advance. To make sure your budget is reasonable, find out what the average cost of your destinations is.

9. Currency Conversion Apps

To keep up with exchange rates, download currency conversion apps. This enables you to exchange money or make purchases with knowledge.

Staying Connected: SIM Cards and Wi-Fi

1. Local SIM Cards

Invest in a local SIM card to get your connectivity going. Visit approved mobile providers, such as AT&T, Movistar, or Telcel, to select a plan that best suits your calling and data requirements.

2. Compatible Phones

To use a local SIM card in Mexico, make sure your phone is unlocked before traveling there. To ensure smooth communication, confirm compatibility with Mexican networks and frequencies.

3. Wi-Fi Availability

Hotels, cafes, tourist destinations, and urban areas are all common places to find Wi-Fi. Use the free Wi-Fi to stay connected for online activities, messaging, and navigation.

4. Portable Wi-Fi Devices

For on-the-go connectivity, think about renting a portable Wi-Fi device (Mi-Fi). These gadgets guarantee that you're always connected by offering a dependable and safe internet connection for numerous devices.

5. International Roaming

Inquire about your options for international roaming with your home mobile provider. Although this can be convenient, be mindful that the costs could be very high.

In order to prevent unforeseen fees, think about disabling data roaming.

6. Messaging Apps and WhatsApp

Use messaging apps such as Telegram, Signal, or WhatsApp to make free voice, text, and video calls using Wi-Fi. Maintain free communication with loved ones without paying extra.

7. VPN for Security

When utilizing public Wi-Fi networks, install a Virtual Private Network (VPN) for increased security. This guarantees a safe online experience and protects your data.

8. Internet Cafés

Many Mexican cities have access to internet cafés. These can be practical choices if you need to use a computer or the internet for a brief period of time.

9. Acquire Data Bundles

Various data packages are available from mobile carriers. Analyze how much data you use and choose a plan that suits your requirements. Using this to stay connected while visiting could be economical.

10. Offline Maps

Use apps like Google Maps to download offline maps so you can navigate without using data. This is especially useful when traveling through places with spotty internet.

11. Interact with Locals

Talk to locals to find out where Wi-Fi hotspots are and what the best connectivity options are. They can offer insightful advice on how to remain in touch in their area.

EXPLORING NATURE: MOUNTAINS, BEACHES, AND BEYOND

Top Hiking Trails

1. Copper Canyon Trails (Sierra Tarahumara)

Discover the captivating Copper Canyon, a larger and deeper network of canyons than the Grand Canyon. For breathtaking views, hike the Urique Canyon trail or take a trip down the Batopilas Canyon.

2. Toluca Nevado

Explore the paths of the dormant volcano Nevado de Toluca, which is home to two breathtaking crater lakes. The strenuous but worthwhile hike provides sweeping views of the surrounding mountains and alpine scenery.

3. Parque Nacional Cumbres de Monterrey

Follow the paths in this naturalist's paradise, Cumbres de Monterrey National Park. Opt for routes such as the strenuous hike to Cerro de la Silla or the Chipinque Ecotourism Park.

4. Pico de Orizaba

Climb Pico de Orizaba, the highest peak in Mexico. Ascending the nation's most famous volcano, the trails take you through rocky terrain and alpine meadows while providing you with unmatched views.

5. Sierra Gorda Biosphere Reserve

Take in Sierra Gorda's verdant surroundings. Explore the biosphere reserve's trails to find waterfalls, caves, and a variety of plants and animals.

6. Hierve el Agua Trails

Explore the trails that encircle this bizarre location of petrified waterfalls. Take in the expansive vistas of the Oaxacan valleys and lose yourself in the distinctive geological structures.

7. El Chico National Park

Experience the splendor of El Chico National Park, renowned for its enchanting rock formations and forests. Trek the paths that lead to La Peña del Cuervo to get breathtaking views of the surroundings.

8. Sierra Nevada de Santa Marta

Explore the Chiapas region's Sierra Nevada de Santa Marta, which is endowed with a variety of ecosystems. Scale Cerro El Baúl to get views of cloud forests, waterfalls, and prehistoric Mayan ruins.

9. Sierra de San Pedro Martír

Traverse the paths of Baja California's Sierra de San Pedro Martír National Park. The Picacho del Diablo trail is difficult but offers a rewarding summit experience, and the park is home to a diverse range of plants and animals.

10. Malinche Volcano Trails

Take on the trails of La Malinche, a prominent summit dormant volcano. The trails offer opportunities for hikers of all skill levels, from beginners to experts.

Best Scuba Diving Hotspots

1. Cozumel

Discover the well-known reefs that encircle the Caribbean island of Cozumel. Experience a rainbow of coral formations, sea fans, and interactions with marine life, including turtles and nurse sharks, at the Palancar and Columbia Reef systems.

2. Cenotes of the Riviera Maya

Take a deep dive into these mysterious underground pools. Explore stalactite and stalagmite-adorned underwater tunnels and caverns. Famous cenote dive sites Dos Ojos and Gran Cenote provide a distinctive underwater experience.

3. Socorro Islands

See amazing encounters with massive pelagic species by traveling to the isolated Socorro Islands in the Pacific Ocean. In these open-ocean waters, go diving with hammerhead sharks, manta rays, and even the elusive whale shark.

4. Cabo Pulmo National Marine Park

Enter the thriving Cabo Pulmo National Marine Park, recognized as a World Heritage Site by UNESCO. Observe the astounding comeback of the aquatic fauna, encompassing vast shoals of fish, sea lions, and bull sharks.

5. Isla Mujeres

Known for its crystal-clear waters and varied marine ecosystems, explore the underwater wonders of Isla Mujeres. Popular dive sites rich in vibrant marine life include the Manchones Reef and the Cave of the Sleeping Sharks.

6. Guadalupe Island

Known for shark encounters, Guadalupe Island offers unique diving experiences. Experience an amazing cage dive with great white sharks in the pristine waters, making memories with these top predators.

7. Banco Chinchorro

Explore Banco Chinchorro, the biggest coral atoll in the Northern Hemisphere. Discover shipwrecks and coral gardens while taking in this marine reserve's abundant biodiversity.

8. Isla Holbox

Take a dive in the island's crystal-clear waters to possibly spot whale sharks. For an incredible experience, snorkel or dive with these kinds of giants during their migratory season.

9. Puerto Morelos

Explore the Mesoamerican Barrier Reef System by diving in Puerto Morelos. Discover the variety of coral formations and get up close with colorful reef fish, rays, and seahorses.

Best Bird Watching Spots

1. Reserva de la Biosfera Ría Lagartos

Enjoy the sight of flamingos swimming in the shallow waters of Yucatán's Ría Lagartos Biosphere Reserve. See a variety of shorebirds, herons, and egrets against the backdrop of mangroves.

2. El Triunfo Biosphere Reserve

Take a deep breath and explore Chiapas' cloud forests at El Triunfo Biosphere Reserve. Discover rare species in this bird paradise, such as the Emerald Toucanet, the Resplendent Quetzal, and a variety of hummingbirds.

3. Celestún Biosphere Reserve

Explore the Yucatán region's mangroves and wetlands. See the vivid pink colors of flamingos, as well as ibises, boat-billed herons, and other waterfowl.

4. Sumidero Canyon National Park

Travel through Chiapas's breathtaking Sumidero Canyon, where kingfishers skitter along the riverbanks and eagles soar overhead. The elusive Bare-throated Tiger Heron is something to look for.

5. Monarch Butterfly Biosphere Reserve

Visit Michoacán's Monarch Butterfly Biosphere Reserve to combine birdwatching and butterfly viewing. As the trees are covered in monarch butterflies, pay attention to the calls of woodland birds such as vireos and warblers.

6. Sierra Gorda Biosphere Reserve

Explore Sierra Gorda's varied terrain in Querétaro. Amidst the verdant forests and rough terrain, spot graceful trogons, vibrant orioles, and the critically endangered military macaw.

MEXICO FOR FAMILIES

Top Family-Friendly Destinations

1. Cancún and Playa del Carmen

Enjoy the lively nightlife, family-friendly beaches, and neighboring eco-parks like Xcaret. Explore historic Mayan ruins, go diving in crystal-clear waters, and savor regional cuisine.

2. Puerto Vallarta

Take in the allure of Puerto Vallarta's bustling Malecón, water sports, and resorts that are suitable for families.

Explore the town's art scene or go on a boat tour to the Marietas Islands.

3. Riviera Maya

Take your family to experience Riviera Maya's breathtaking natural beauty. Explore the eco-adventures of Xplor Park, swim in cenotes, and tour the historic ruins of Tulum.

4. Mexico City

Uncover Mexico City's rich history and culture. Take a boat ride in Xochimilco, explore museums like the National Museum of Anthropology, and go to Chapultepec Park.

5. Oaxaca

Take pleasure in the lively hues and rich cultural customs of Oaxaca. Take a leisurely stroll through the quaint city center, visit a nearby market, and enroll in kid-friendly cooking classes.

6. Cabo San Lucas

Unwind on the beaches that receive an abundance of sunlight. Enjoy water sports, go on a boat tour to El Arco, and check out the town's family-friendly attractions.

7. Playa del Carmen

Savor the vibrant ambiance of Playa del Carmen. Take a stroll down Fifth Avenue, take in the beaches, and go on family-friendly trips to neighboring attractions.

8. Tulum

Take in Tulum's bohemian charm. Take the family on eco-friendly adventures, unwind on immaculate beaches, and explore the archaeological site.

9. Guanajuato

Immerse yourself in Guanajuato's colonial beauty. Take a funicular ride for sweeping views, explore the historic city center, and visit museums like the Diego Rivera House.

10. Huatulco

Unwind in Huatulco's laid-back atmosphere. Explore the picturesque bays and coves, go snorkeling, and discover the family-friendly beaches of this Pacific paradise.

Best Kid-Friendly Activities

1. Xcaret Park - Riviera Maya

Take your family to Xcaret, an eco-archaeological park, and experience its wonders. Take in the vivid flora and fauna, swim in underground rivers, and watch cultural performances.

2. Interactive Museums in Mexico City

Take a look around kid-friendly museums that offer interactive exhibits and educational experiences, like the Museo Interactivo de Economía and the Papalote Museo del Niño.

3. Yucatán Peninsula Cenote Snorkeling

Take your family snorkeling in the Peninsula's glistening cenotes. Discover submerged caverns and be amazed by the distinctive geological structures.

4. Whale Watching - Baja California

Take the whole family on a whale-watching trip in Baja California. Observe the magnificent gray whales as they journey each year.

5. Chichen Itzá Light and Sound Show

The family-friendly Chichen Itzá Light and Sound Show offers an opportunity to immerse yourself in the enchantment of the city. See the vibrant illuminations and historical stories about the Mayans bringing the ancient ruins to life.

6. Chapultepec Castle in Mexico City

For sweeping views, ascend to the summit of Chapultepec Castle in Mexico City. Take a boat ride on the lake, explore the castle grounds, and go to the Chapultepec Zoo.

7. Xel-Há Park - Riviera Maya

Explore Xel-Há Park's aquatic adventures. Discover the park's natural cenotes, float down languid rivers, and go snorkeling with tropical fish.

8. Interactive Aquarium - Cancún

Take a trip to the Interactive Aquarium in Cancún, where kids can interact with interactive exhibits and have exhilarating experiences with dolphins to get up close and personal with marine life.

9. Mayan Adventure Park - Costa Maya

Visit Costa Maya and go on a Mayan adventure. Take part in educational activities about Mayan culture, zip-line through the jungle, and examine replicas of ancient structures.

10. Veracruz Papantla Flyers

See the captivating Papantla Flyers ceremony in Veracruz. See a customary ceremony that enthralls spectators of all ages as artists spiral down from a tall pole.

Made in the USA
Las Vegas, NV
16 January 2024